The Soccer Star

Joshua Mitchell

Illustrated by Margaret Power

"My favorite soccer player is on TV!
I want to be a soccer star, too," I said.

"You need to be fit to be
a good soccer player," said Dad.
"You need lots of exercise."

"I'm going to exercise every day!"
I said.

"I'll help you!" said Mai.
"There are lots of ways to exercise."

"Let's take the dog to the park," said Mai.

"That does not sound like exercise," I said.

"Wait and see!" said Mai.

“This is a fun way to get fit!” I said.

"Let's play hopscotch," said Mai.

"That does not sound like exercise," I said.

"Wait and see!" said Mai.

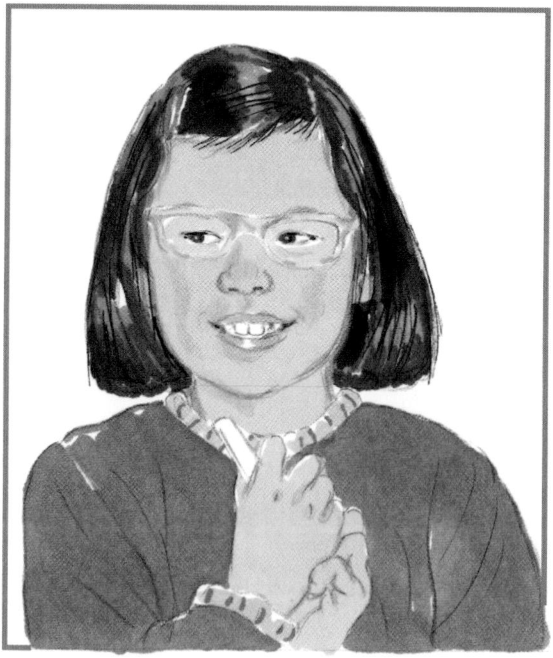

“This is a fun way to get fit!” I said.

"Let's help Mom in the garden,"
said Mai.

"That does not sound like exercise,"
I said.

"Wait and see!" said Mai.

“This is a fun way to get fit!” I said.

"Let's help Dad with the groceries," said Mai.

"That will be exercise, too!" I said.

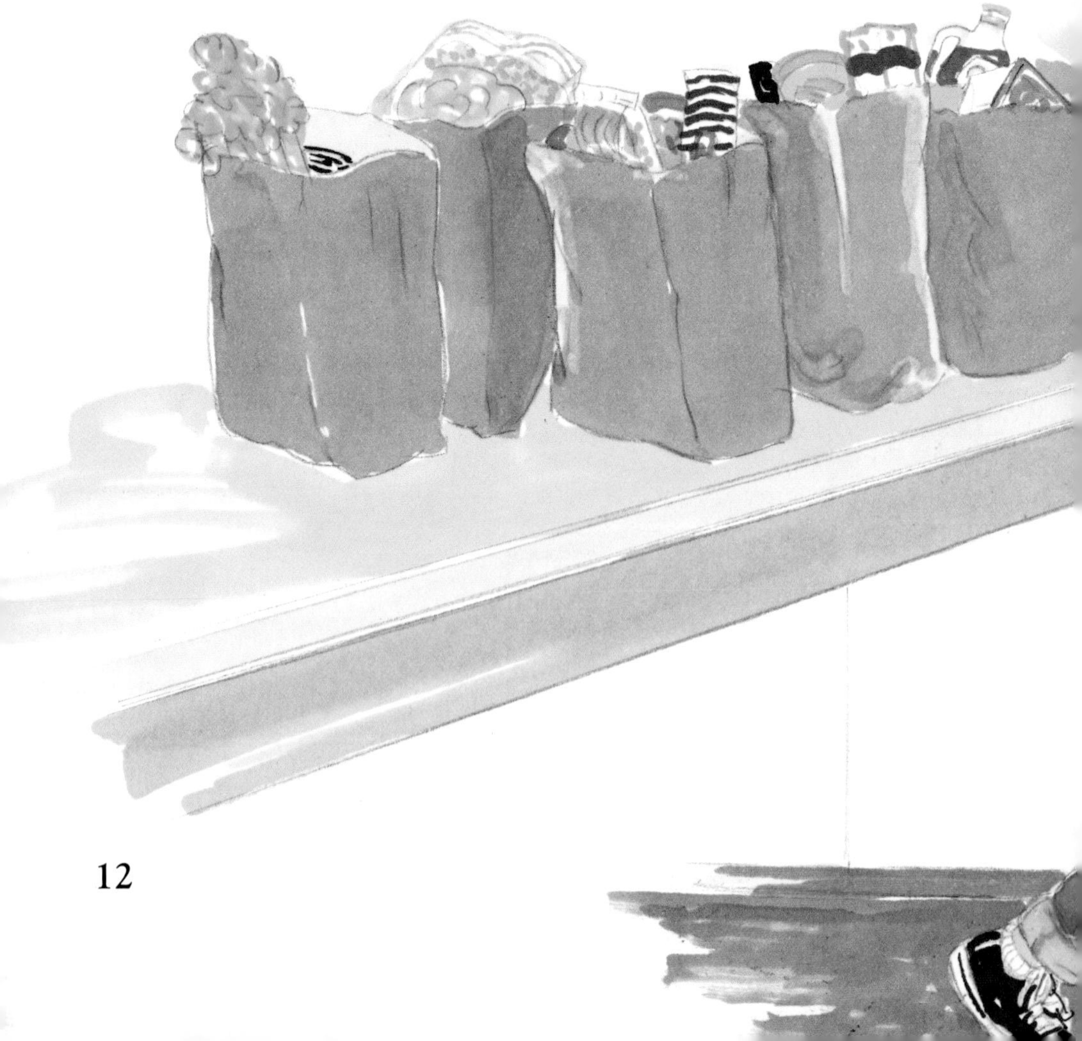

"You exercised a lot this week,"
said Mai.

"You will be a soccer star soon!
There's just one more thing
you need," said Dad.

"A soccer ball!"

"Thanks, Dad!" I said.